A Minute with Mom

Weekly Affirmations with Teen Daughter

APRIL SPANN

ISBN 978-1-0980-9792-9 (paperback)
ISBN 978-1-0980-9793-6 (digital)

Christian Faith Publishing, Inc.
832 Park Avenue
Meadville, PA 16335
www.christianfaithpublishing.com

Printed in the United States of America

To my daughter, Laela Necole. You are such a joy and inspiration. Always be who God has called you to be. Continue to walk in your purpose and remember: Mama loves you!

TABLE OF CONTENTS

Coloring Page

Each weekday morning, I would send my daughter a text right before school to let her know I was thinking of her, love her, and wanted her to have some inspiration to start off her day. My text messages were filled with hearts, butterflies, and other emoticons to grab her attention and to encourage her to keep reading even though I knew she would. To my surprise, she had asked me why I stopped.

She enjoyed reading them. That remark became the inspiration for this journal. We, as mothers, want to give our daughters just a little minute with us where there are no interruptions and we can pour into them all that God has given us to share.

This journal includes the following:

- twenty prayers for mom and daughter to discuss together, draw inspirations, and begin everyday moments between them
- weekly reminders
- a self-care section
- seven positive affirmations
- notes/reflection section
- fun coloring pages

Know Your Worth!

Know your worth! You are *far more* valuable than anything on this earth! You are priceless! You *cannot* be bought or swayed especially with cheap jewelry or anything materialistic for that matter.

To God be the glory that others have recognized your value. But do not let others take you down a road that you never intended to be on. God wants more for you. I want better for you. Make better choices. Be sure you are leading others around you. We are Royalty!

Remember: Mama loves you!

For her worth is far above jewels.
(Proverbs 31:10)

Notes

_____

_____

_____

_____

_____

_____

_____

_____

_____

_____

_____

_____

_____

_____

For her worth is far above jewels.
(Proverbs 31:10)

Know Whose You Are!

Know whose you are! It is no mistake that you know you are my daughter. We practically look identical! It is such a blessing and a joy to call you my daughter! But other than our similarities, there is one that you should be like every day. You guessed it—Christ! Of course, you know that is serious business. And it should not be taken lightly.

It is undeniable that you belong to the body of Christ. I know you understand that, but I want to make sure we can discuss all things that affect you. Continue to walk with the Lord and look to Him for guidance in all matters. We are available too, obviously. Smile!

Christ is the foundation on which everything we do! He is our identity! Yes, we should strive to look like Him more and more each day. Do not take it for granted!

Remember: Mama loves you!

Let no one boast in men. And you belong to Christ; and Christ belongs to God.
(1 Corinthians 3:21-23)

Notes

_____

_____

_____

_____

_____

_____

_____

_____

_____

_____

_____

_____

_____

Let no one boast in men. And you belong to
Christ; and Christ belongs to God.
(1 Corinthians 3:21-23)

Know We Radiate Christ!

Know we radiate Christ! Yes, you are beautiful. But more importantly than outward appearances, we are made in Christ's image. His light should radiate through every fiber of our being. He dwells within us. We should be so bright because of His shining presence within us that others ask, *What are you using?* Your skin, your persona, your vibe is glowing through you!

Are you reflecting Christ's image around your school friends or only your church friends? Never change. Be who you are with everyone. It is less tiring!

Again, do not let others take you on a road that you never intended to be on. Do not let anyone take you off course. Be a leader in all situations and show nonbelievers the Christ that is inside of you.

Remember: Mama loves you!

Let your light shine before others, that they may see your good deeds and glorify your Father in heaven.
(Matthew 5:16)

Notes

_____

_____

_____

_____

_____

_____

_____

_____

_____

_____

_____

_____

_____

Let your light shine before others, that they
may see your good deeds and glorify your
Father in heaven.
(Matthew 5:16)

Stay Humble

Stay humble. Now what exactly does that mean? We hear it enough from others, but do you know it means to walk humbly and not boast or be arrogant?

Do not get me wrong, you are doing amazingly awesome at school and with extracurricular activities. I am so proud of you! I also know that God has VERY BIG PLANS for you, and that is a blessing! You have a very special gifting inside of you. Stay in prayer. Be obedient about it.

Be mindful of your actions. God is always watching. Again, do not let others take you off your course in life. God wants more for you. I want better for you. Always think through your choices.

Remember: Mama loves you!

Therefore, humble yourselves under the mighty hand of God, that He may exalt you at the proper time.
(1 Peter 5:6)

Notes

_____

_____

_____

_____

_____

_____

_____

_____

_____

_____

_____

_____

_____

_____

Therefore, humble yourselves under the
mighty hand of God, that He may exalt you
at the proper time.
(1 Peter 5:6)

You Can Do Anything!

You can *do* anything! *Yes*, you *can do* anything! You are very smart! You are exactly who God intended you to be! How amazing is that! There is so much promise and purpose in that affirmation! No one can take that away from you. Whatever you set your mind to, *do it*! And do it with God standing by your side. I believe in your abilities. I know you are destined to do greater things. Trust in the Lord with all your heart and watch Him show out in your life! Are you excited? I AM!

Greater things are yet to be revealed in your purpose-driven walk with Christ.

Remember: Mama loves you!

I can do all things through
Christ who strengthens me.
(Philippians 4:13)

Notes

I can do all things through
Christ who strengthens me.
(Philippians 4:13)

Coloring Page

WEEKLY REMINDERS
Pray Daily. Live for God.

Prayer Requests

_____

_____

_____

Answered Prayers

_____

_____

_____

Notes

_____

_____

_____

I can do all things through Christ who
strengthens me.
(Philippians 4:13)

Love Yourself More! #1

Love yourself more! What do I mean by that? I simply mean for you to love yourself more by being in tune with the things around you. Loving who you see each and every morning when you look in the mirror.

Love yourself more by

- taking care of the things you can control like your surroundings. Make sure you are not involved in any activity that would cause you harm or anyone around you.
- choosing your friends wisely. Be mindful of the friends who you allow to share your personal space.
- letting go of toxic behaviors and/or people. Negativity only weighs on you. Remove yourself from it.

When you love who you are in the mirror (or out), you will love the beautiful person God created. You would love your funny quirks, your silliness, your loud laughter. Simply put, loving *you!*

Remember: Mama loves you!

I will give thanks to You, for I am fearfully and wonderfully made; Wonderful are Your works, And my soul knows it very well.
(Psalms 139:14)

Let's Talk about It: Watch

Watch: Be protective of your eyes.

You wear sunglasses, right? If you do not, you should! They protect you from the harmful sun's rays. As such, you should protect your eyes from ungodly mess. Do not be so ready to see or read what your friends are doing, downloading the latest gossip. Be mindful of what you bring into your vision.

Your eyes are very important. God has gifted you with the ability to see. They influence you to go one direction or another because of what you have seen. With your eyes, you bring light into your body. If you give them what is pure and holy, they can lead you to see the wonders of God. Your eyes should be protected. You should not use them to see worldly behaviors such as explicit or vulgar behaviors.

This is important because the more you watch the wrong thing, the likelihood it can enter your heart. And there is just no space for that because your heart is full on Jesus!

Remember: Mama loves you!

The eye is the lamp of the body.
(Matthew 6:22)

Notes

The eye is the lamp of the body.
(Matthew 6:22)

Let's Talk about It: Wash

Wash: Wash your mouth out!

It is filled with germs! Yuck! Your speech/attitude/body language is concerning when disciplined, but your mouth needs a washing. Do not let your back talk and attitude keep you away from your blessings because you failed to wash your mouth out!

How do you wash your mouth out? Wash daily with the Word of God. Do not let a bad attitude steal what God has for you. Bad attitudes can lead to how you speak to others around you. This can lead to patterns and behavior changes. It can become a really big deal if you let it creep into your life.

Washing your mouth out also includes brushing your teeth. Every girl has to, needs to, wants to look their best for the day if not for no one but themselves. Never walk out of the house without making sure you have done all you can for: (1) God, our Father (your morning prayer); (2) yourself.

AGAIN, take care of 1 and 2 everyday!

Remember: Mama loves you!

Let no unwholesome word proceed from your mouth, but only such a word as is good for edification according to the need of the moment, so that it will give grace to those who hear.
(Ephesians 4:29)

Notes

_____

_____

_____

_____

_____

_____

_____

_____

_____

_____

Let no unwholesome word proceed from your
mouth, but only such a word as is good for
edification according to the need of the moment,
so that it will give grace to those who hear.
(Ephesians 4:29)

Let's Talk about It: Wear

Wear: Always be presentable!

You are made in Christ's image, so who are you reflecting when you are unpresentable? Yes, you still reflect Christ. Because you have taken a stand for Christ and others know it, you are now "judged" by your actions and how you carry yourself.

Are you someone others want to imitate? Are you reflecting Christ in the highest regards at any given time? Others see you and want to look up to you. Be sure to lead others down the right path, which leads them directly to Christ.

Skimpy clothing is not who we are or what we are about. This can lead to temptation and other areas that are not pleasing to God. Always know: as girls, we carry ourselves with high standards.

As a reminder, do not let others take you down a road that you never intended to be on. God wants more for you.

Always think through your choices.

Remember: Mama loves you!

God created man in His own image.
(Genesis 1:27)

Notes

God created man in His own image.
(Genesis 1:27)

You Are God's Magnificent Creation

You are God's magnificent creation! Say what? You are created in the likeness of God! That is shouting news right there! No one can take that away from you. You are price-less! You are God's craftsmanship. You are beautifully made! God crafted you while you were inside of me. He placed every single hair on your head. God was intentional with forming you. What a blessing!

Do not let other girls take your confidence away. Do not let them get in your head with lies or jealous comments. You respond to the haters with kindness, love, and prayer. Be sure you keep your inner circle of friends close. That means everyone does not have to walk in your inner circle, and no one needs to know everything that you do. Everyone around you is not your friend.

Some people want to see you fail. Some people want to see you in places other than where God intends you to be. Rise above that noise. Seek first the kingdom of God. Turn your haters over to God!

Remember: Mama loves you!

Before I formed you in the womb, I knew you.
(Jeremiah 1:5)

Notes

_____

_____

_____

_____

_____

_____

_____

_____

_____

_____

_____

_____

_____

_____

_____

_____

Before I formed you in the womb, I knew you.
(Jeremiah 1:5)

Choose Joy, Not Happiness

Choose JOY not happiness. Why would I say choose joy instead of happiness? It seems as if happiness is the best answer to everyday living. But in actuality, happiness is a temporary smile. One day your smile is right side up, the next, it is upside down. It is ever-changing. Happiness is being silly, being giddy, being funny. It is a state of being.

Joy, on the other hand, is constant. It is sustained. You have joy. You choose joy. Our sustained joy is rooted and centered in Christ! He is the source of our joy! This joy allows us to smile in the midst of the craziness all around us. It is because of Christ that we find ourselves being joyful just because we know God has a plan for our lives.

When we choose to let Jesus rule over us, the joy and peace found in that choice is everlasting. It is sustained. We do not have to make any decisions on our own. Jesus carries that load for us. We have to trust Him and turn our loads over to Him. It is comforting to know that we have someone in our corner that we can turn our innermost problems over to. That is joyful news!

Remember: Mama loves you!

For the joy of the Lord is my strength.
(Nehemiah 8:10)

Notes

_____

_____

_____

_____

_____

_____

_____

_____

_____

_____

_____

_____

_____

For the joy of the Lord is my strength.
(Nehemiah 8:10)

Coloring Page

WEEKLY REMINDERS

Pray Daily. Love Your Neighbor.

Prayer Requests

_____

_____

_____

Answered Prayers

_____

_____

_____

Notes

_____

_____

_____

For the joy of the Lord is my strength.
(Nehemiah 8:10)

You Are Talented!

You are talented! I am SUPER proud of you! God has given you tremendous talents. He has given you specific skills to accomplish His will with your life. You have taken His direction and ran with it!

You have many things on your plate, and you are still performing at a high level. Please make sure you do not get the BIG head. Smile! Getting too BIG of yourself can lead to destruction. Stay grounded. Stay humble.

Remember to give your all to every endeavor you begin. Give God the glory for it all and have fun!

Remember: Mama loves you!

For we are God's workmanship, created in
Christ Jesus for good works, which God
prepared beforehand so that we would walk
in them.
(Ephesians 2:10)

Notes

For we are God's workmanship, created in
Christ Jesus for good works, which God
prepared beforehand so that we would walk
in them.
(Ephesians 2:10)

Coloring Page

Positive Role Models

Positive Role Models. This is a big one! Why? Because depending on what you think determines where you place your attention. Role models—who are they to you? You have said that you think role models are the perfect example of who you look up to. Yes, I can agree with that definition. Role models are examples that anyone can look up to, to imitate. Since they are important influencers, you should make sure you choose your role models wisely.

The world would have you to believe that celebrities are great examples of who a role model should be. But of course, we know better!

There is no reason that you cannot admire someone. Admiration means that you have respect for someone. Admire them for their accomplishments. Admire them for their charity work. Admire them for overcoming their obstacles.

But role models? They are more personal, wouldn't you say? If they are to influence any decision you make, you need to be sure you have positive role models (examples) in your life. Remember, we are made in the image of Christ. There is only one perfect example, and that is Christ. When you think of imitating people, choose those who imitate Christ. Your role models should be Christ-representers who represents Christ in their actions. Something to think about.

Remember: Mama loves you!

Be imitators of me, just as I also am of
Christ.
(1 Corinthians 11:1)

Notes

_____

_____

_____

_____

_____

_____

_____

_____

_____

_____

_____

_____

_____

_____

_____

_____

_____

Be imitators of me, just as I also am of
Christ.
(1 Corinthians 11:1)

KEEP GOING

I Feel Like a Failure

I feel like a failure! So, you are upset! This was not your best week. Nothing panned out as you had planned. It is okay to feel bummed about it. It is a necessary emotion. But what are you going to do about it? What actions will you take to put yourself in a different position so that you do not have the same outcome as before? You must position yourself to win. How do you do that? You study more, you play harder, you do your best. You also learn from this and move forward. Never give up. You put in the work to excel so you are not back in the same spot.

Keep in mind: winning is not everything. Would you agree? I know it sucks if you are losing, have lost your game or hit the wrong note. You put in the work, you practiced hard, and you still failed. It happens like that sometimes. But you keep trying and try some more until you master it!

You can do all things through Christ, but you never give up. It is okay to have bad days, but do not stress out. Learn from it, and keep it moving forward. It is how you respond to failures in life. Learn and grow from them, understand the lesson in midst of defeat. It stings, but in the end, you WIN!

    Work at it.

    In spite of obstacles,

    Never give up!

Remember: Mama loves you!

Do you not know that those who run in a race all run, but only one receives the prize? Run in such a way that you may win. (1 Corinthians 9:24)

Notes

Do you not know that those who run in
a race all run, but only one receives the
prize? Run in such a way that you may win.
(1 Corinthians 9:24)

Surround Yourself with Like-Minded Friends

Surround yourself with like-minded friends. What does that mean? You may say you like all of your friends. That may be true, and that is okay. But as you continue to grow in the things of Christ, you will need to have people around you who think like you do. People who hold the same values as you. People who regard the same things as important to them just like they are important to you.

When you begin to do this, you will have people in your inner circle who only want the best for you. These people will hold you accountable on things you both hold dear.

Remember: Mama loves you!

He who walks with wise men will be wise, But the companion of fools will suffer harm. (Proverbs 13:20)

Notes

He who walks with wise men will
be wise, But the companion of fools
will suffer harm. (Proverbs 13:20)

I AM A CHILD OF
GOD

Serve

Serve. Always be of service to others, but be careful that you are serving not to be seen but with a genuine heart. What does that mean? It means to have the right motives when you are serving God's people—It means to have a servant's heart and care about what you are doing. Jesus came to serve not to be served. Serve like Christ.

While serving others is important, it is most important that you serve God with your life. What? That means live your life in a way that glorifies God. Your life should make God smile and be proud to call you daughter. This does not mean that you will not make bad decisions or that trouble will not come, but when it does, turn your situations, problems, concerns over to God.

He will handle them every time.

You must first build a consistent relationship with Him so that you will always know when and how He responds to your needs. Serve Him by consistently reading and doing what His word says, which directs your path. Serve Him by turning your life over to Him. He will direct your path. He will show you the way forward. How exciting is that? You do not have to worry about what to do next. God will guide you. Serve Him in your conduct. Serve Him faithfully. Serve Him daily.

Remember: Mama loves you!

Train up a child in the way he should go, Even when he is old, he will not depart from it. (Proverbs 22:6)

Notes

_____

_____

_____

_____

_____

_____

_____

_____

_____

_____

_____

_____

_____

_____

Train up a child in the way he should
go, Even when he is old, he will not
depart from it. (Proverbs 22:6)

Coloring Page

WEEKLY REMINDERS
Pray Daily. Enjoy Life.

Prayer Requests

_____

_____

_____

Answered Prayers

_____

_____

_____

Notes

_____

_____

_____

Train up a child in the way he should
go, Even when he is old, he will not
depart from it. (Proverbs 22:6)

Love Yourself More #2

Love yourself more! Even more! Well, how can you do that? I simply mean for you to take care of yourself. Let's take a moment to discuss the three big hygiene areas. They are personal hygiene, dental hygiene, and wearing clean clothes daily.

These are three of many daily responsibilities everyone has. By making sure your hygiene is top notch, you avoid sickness and also others viewing you negatively. You feel good. You smell good. You look good. Your demeanor changes or improves.

You are ready to take on your day. Good hygiene can boost your self-esteem.

Remember: Mama loves you!

Notes

Let's Talk about Hygiene: Personal

Personal Hygiene

Personal hygiene includes body cleanliness—taking showers/baths thoroughly and daily, wearing deodorant, washing your hands, paying extra special care of your feet.

You are very active in extracurricular activities. Your body is highly responsive to all of the activities that you put it through by sweating.

We, as girls, have to make sure we are clean because we have special areas that need addressing each and every day.

Be mindful to switch your gym shoes every other day to avoid having smelly feet.

Remember: Mama loves you!

Wash yourselves, make yourselves clean.
(Isaiah 1:16)

Notes

_____

_____

_____

_____

_____

_____

_____

_____

_____

_____

_____

_____

_____

_____

Wash yourselves, make yourselves clean.
(Isaiah 1:16)

Let's Talk about Hygiene: Dental

Dental Hygiene

Dental hygiene includes brushing your teeth and flossing regularly to avoid bad breath and bad teeth. I want to make sure you have healthy gums and a healthy smile. I know you love your sweets and soft drinks! Those things are good in moderation. That means you can enjoy them in small doses. You should not eat or drink them on a regular basis. You also cannot leave that sugar on your teeth. You must take care of your teeth. I want to make sure you have teeth when you get older. I understand you know these things, but some things bear repeating just to make sure.

Smile.

Brushing daily, preferably twice a day, removes bacteria from your teeth that can cause bad breath. Bacteria can lead to gingivitis and cavities. Flossing removes bacteria from between your teeth. Floss daily.

Remember: Mama loves you!

A cheerful heart brings a smile to your face.
(Proverbs 15:13)

Notes

_____
_____
_____
_____
_____
_____
_____
_____
_____
_____
_____
_____
_____

A cheerful heart brings a smile to your face.
(Proverbs 15:13)

Let's Talk about Hygiene: Cleanliness

Cleanliness

Always wear clean clothes. Wearing dirty clothes can cause unpleasant, smelly situations. When you leave gym class, change your clothes. Dirty clothes and/or body odors can bring unwanted attention to you and can cause teasing from those around you.

Practicing good hygiene allows you to have friends in your inner circle and not be afraid of catching germs. Many germs lie in unclean areas. You want to make sure you are doing everything you can to stay so fresh and so clean.

Remember: Mama loves you!

Then I will sprinkle clean water on you, and you will be clean.
(Ezekiel 36:25)

Notes

Then I will sprinkle clean water on you, and
you will be clean.
(Ezekiel 36:25)

Read and Do!

Read and do! What do I mean by that? I simply mean for you to read your Bible daily, and after you read it, do what it says. Simple, right?

It is not enough to simply read the Word of God. Even an unbeliever can read the Word of God. We, as believers, must be actively doing what His Word instructs us to do.

I understand that there is a lot going on in your life right now—school, commitments, extracurricular activities. But do not forget to spend time in God's Word. You must build a strong relationship with God. Your relationship with Christ builds your foundation for a lasting walk with God.

Reading His Word daily is how He talks to you. You talk to Him through prayer. His Word gives advice, directs your path, and sets you up for the win.

Remember: Mama loves you!

Do not merely listen to the word, and so deceive yourselves. Do what it says.
(James 1:22)

Notes

Do not merely listen to the word, and so
deceive yourselves. Do what it says.
(James 1:22)

Coloring Page

Honor Your Father and Mother

Honor your father and mother. Honor your father and your mother as it is one of the Ten Commandments. Simply put, respect your parents. Respect the authority that God has given them over your well-being.

Ways to honor your parents:

- *Honor by being respectful.* **Parents ask a lot of their kids. We want and expect you to do great things. Do not use a disrespectful tone in your voice. Often times, it is how you say it, not what you say that can be mistaken as being disrespectful.**
- *Honor with your words.* **Do not talk or mutter under your breath. Do not talk back after we have spoken to you. Do not have an attitude.**
- *Honor by not rolling your eyes.* **We see you. Your eyes tell us how you really feel. Rolling your eyes when asked to do something is a direct indication that your disrespectful**

level is on high alert! Be mindful of your body tone.

If this seems to be an area that needs work, talk to God. Ask for help. He can guide you through these times when you do not know how to communicate your feelings. Simply talk to God. Simply talk to your parents.

Remember: Mama loves you!

Honor them so that your days may be prolonged
(Exodus 20:12).

Notes

_____

_____

_____

_____

_____

_____

_____

_____

_____

_____

_____

_____

_____

Honor them so that your days may be
prolonged
(Exodus 20:12).

WEEKLY REMINDERS

Pray Daily. Get Your Rest.

Prayer Requests

_____

_____

_____

Answered Prayers

_____

_____

_____

Notes

_____

_____

_____

Honor them so that your days may be
prolonged
(Exodus 20:12).

Self-Care Section

This section is here to give you some tips on what you can do daily to take care of yourself. Tips that focuses on your emotional, mental, and overall health. These tips can also reduce the amount of stress you face and empower you to face your day with confidence.

- Prayer—I would encourage you to begin and end your day with prayer. This is a great way to give whatever that is on your mind over to the One who can answer your smallest request. That is Jesus!
- Play with your pet—This is a great stress reliever and really fun to do!
- Color/Draw/Paint—Fun activity!
- Rest—Do you need to recharge? Be sure to get the right amount of sleep/rest each day.
- Self-reflect—Reflect on your day! What areas can you improve on?
- Exercise/walk—Get your heart rate up!
- Play Sports—Enjoy your friends.
- Read—Quiet time to read.
- Sing/Play/Listen to Music—Fun activities.

Notes

Seven Positive Affirmations

These affirmations are positive reinforcements to remind you that your inner beauty is very important, to empower you to reach your goals, and to achieve your God-given purpose.

In your quiet time, speak these affirmations aloud. Listen intently to what you are saying. Believe that you can do all things through Christ who strengthens you.

1. *I am fearfully and wonderfully made.* There is no other like me. God made me beautifully, a one-of-a-kind masterpiece.
2. *I can do all things through Christ* who strengthens me to excel in all things I set out to do.
3. *I am enough.* God has empowered me to be enough for all things that I set out to do.
4. *I will shine.* I will radiate God's love.
5. *I am loved.* God loves me. My family loves me. I am loved.

6. *I am worth it.* God intentionally created me. Each hair on my head was created just for me. I belong in the space I walk in.

7. *I am bold in Christ.* God gives me the strength to walk in boldness because I know I belong where He guides me.

Remember You're
AWESOME
UNIQUE • WONDERFULLY MADE • LOVED

Reflections

Reflections

Reflections

Reflections

Reflections

About the Author

April Spann is an author, wife, mother, businesswoman, and motivator. Passionate about motivating women and teen girls, she enjoys ministering when and wherever the Lord leads.

As the owner of G.L.A.M. (God Loves All of Me) Ministries, which inspires teenaged girls to love themselves as they are because they are fearfully and wonderfully made by God, April pursues God's assignments with prayer and dedication.

April, a native Mississippian, accepted Christ as her Savior as a teenager. She and her family are active members of their local church where she is an ordained deaconess. She and her husband, Sylvester Jr., have been married since 2002. They are the proud parents of two teenaged children. She resides in the North Dallas area.

CPSIA information can be obtained
at www.ICGtesting.com
Printed in the USA
BVHW060913221121
622229BV00019B/762